Business Software Development

Principles and Practice

Printed by CreateSpace.

Available from Amazon.com and other online stores.

Available on Kindle and other devices.

First Edition. Published December 2016.

Book details, supporting files, and other book titles can be found at www.antonypennbooks.com

Dedications

To Mum and Dad

This book is dedicated to my Father and to the memory of my Mother, who, from my earliest memories, have always loved and supported me, taught me sound principles and morals, and encouraged me to explore, learn and discover. Without them, I would not be the proud man that I am today, full of desire to explore and improve the world, and appreciative of its wonders. Thank you.

Table of Contents

About this book

Developing software is an expensive, complex business.

This book is intended to advise everyone in the development of software for businesses, with a mix of principles and practices based on traditional wisdom and years of experience.

Although aimed at commercial businesses working on typically small to medium sized projects, either for internal or external client use, many of the principles apply to software development in general.

Unusually for a book such as this, it is not filled with every 'best practice' that you should follow in an ideal world. Instead, it takes a pragmatic approach to what is typically wrong and the essential things you really should follow, in order to get the job done. Time, finance and resource constraints are always against bespoke software development projects. This book offers practical advice to help you make the most of what you have and achieve what you need to.

A lot of the information contained may be considered common sense, but it is important to re-emphasise that knowledge to ourselves from time to time, to ensure we consider it when making decisions. The structure of this book makes it easy to just pick up occasionally and read a few random pages.

This book is organised into sections aimed at the various people involved in the development cycle. However, most of those people would benefit from reading the entire book.

A short software development story

The Big Boss at 'The Company' wants a new version of their 'Product C', to be released at the Event Show in 16 weeks time. There are no specific details yet, so a meeting is arranged between project management and marketing staff to discuss what features should be included.

The development manager is sent the draft specification of the 'version 2' requirements. In those requirements, he notes that the UI design will be coming from an external agency. He asks his main developer if the time-scale can be met, using 2 developers. He needs the answer for a meeting in 2 hours with the Big Boss. The developer says that, at a push, he can get 75% done. The development manager has a meeting with his staff and concludes that, if a third developer joins them from project B when he is finished in 8 weeks time, they can get 90% done, with the remaining 10% moved to a version 2.1 release.

A project kick-off meeting is arranged between the 3 developers, the development manager, the project manager, sales and marketing director and the marketing manager, plus the customer support manager. Due to conflicting schedules, the meeting does not take place for another week.

A project plan is drawn up, together with some milestones. The project is already starting a week later than the developer anticipated, so a few days have been trimmed off the testing phase to make the deadline fit the event date.

The developers start working on a more detailed specification whilst also designing the general structure of the system. They have a few questions that need answering, so the project manager tries to organise a meeting with the sales and marketing staff, but this takes another week to come to fruition. In the meantime, the developers work from their assumptions and start coding.

The UI design does not arrive when expected, so the development manager asks the project manager to talk to his contact at the design company to get an ETA on the designs. A week later they arrive, but there are some issues, so the project manager organises a conference call between himself, the design agency, the development manager and the 3 programmers. This call takes 2 days to occur, but eventually the issues are sorted out and a revised UI design is sent within a few days.

One month into the project is the first milestone date. A meeting is called for everyone involved. It turns out that the project is about a week late. Some minor features are pushed out to release 2.1 in order to give the project time to catch up. A catch-up meeting is planned for 2 weeks time, but again due to conflicting diaries, it is eventually scheduled for 3 weeks time.

At the next review meeting (now 7 weeks into the project), milestone 1 has been met, but the project is still 1 week behind. It is believed that they will catch up, especially as the third developer is due to come on board from Project B next week. Another meeting is scheduled for 3 weeks time, by which time milestone 2 should be met.

At this meeting (10 weeks in) it is discovered that the project is 10 days behind. This is attributed to initial problems with the UI design and the fact that the 3rd developer did not join from Project B when expected, due to problems and delays in that project, plus the second developer keeps getting pulled back to fix bugs with Project A. It is believed the team can catch up, so another progress meeting is planned for all involved in 1 weeks time, where the development team hope to get to milestone 2.

Eleven weeks in and the development team have pulled the

deficit back to 4 days.

The progress meeting held at week 13 discovers that the project is now 8 days behind. The development team did make progress but one of them was sick for a few days. As the initial release date was 4 days before the Event Show, they decide that they can still be ready if they squeeze another day out of the testing and work up until the night before the show, and pull a few late nights. The development manager allows them to order pizza for late nights and gives them the keys to lock up on those nights that developers stay late.

Seven days before the show, and the development team finally ask the project manager, sales and marketing staff, plus some of the support staff to test the product. The original testing phase was 3 weeks plus another week for bug fixes. Staff do not get around to testing the product for 2 days, leaving only 5 days for testing and none for bug fixes.

A few bugs are found and the product is deemed unsuitable for release at the show. The marketing team take it to the show as a 'beta' product and offer 10% off for any pre-orders. A new plan is drawn up by the project manager and the sales and marketing director for the official version 2 release date. The whole cycle starts again.

In the above story, just about every single decision and choice was poor or incorrect, yet it is very likely you have shared many of these same steps and procedures in your own projects. Let's look at why there are wrong and point out some principles that could and should have been used.

Release something by this date

All too often businesses have a date in mind for a project release, yet do not ask the people involved in building that project, how much time they need. Time-scales need to come from developers.

Vague requirements

Many specifications given are very vague, leading to assumptions being made by development staff. Ultimately this will cost more time to correct later, than if it was specified properly up front.

Developers writing specifications

Many specifications arrive at the development department very short on requisite detail. Development or analyst staff should not fill in the gaps themselves, as this leads to assumptions (which results in a broken system taking longer to fix). Instead, work with the client to help them provide the necessary details.

How long will it take?

Developers are often asked to give estimates instantly. This is crazy. You cannot provide a usable estimate without having the time needed to think about it.

Too many stakeholders

Too many people in meetings, are a waste of many people's time, plus cause unnecessary delays whilst trying to find a time suitable for all.

Too many meetings

You need to balance getting the work actually done, against too many meetings talking about it.

The wrong people at meetings

Having the wrong people attend meetings wastes a lot of time. For example, in the story above, there was a conference call between the project manager, external agency, development manager and three programmers, whereas only one programmer and the external agency were required.

Outsource with care

Outsourcing can cause many problems. The first of which is time: you cannot control when they will actually deliver. The second is quality of work: it is much harder to verify quality from afar, especially if work is not delivered continuously.

Revise estimates

After 1 month, this project was 1 week late. You need to look for the reason why and re-calculate the delivery date. Chances are, it will be 4 weeks late after 4 months.

Allow unplanned time

In any project plan, add some time for 'unknown' tasks. Do not put anything in this space. Keep it just for soaking up pressure when deadlines slip. They always do.

Avoid end-to-end planning

If a project or major task finishes on Wednesday, do not plan the next one to start on Thursday. Leave a gap between them to handle overspill. Otherwise, as soon as one thing is late, you will always be late.

Avoid context switching

Programming is a complex task, involving a lot of (human) memory. If a programmer has to switch between project A and project B, he must also 'dump' one project from his mind and 'recall' the second. This is known as a context switch, and costs an awful lot of time. Restrict developers to working on one project at a time as much as possible.

The more developers, the slower

The more developers are working together on a project, the 'slower' (in terms of 'man months' of effort) progress will be, due to increased communication between them.

Plan to lose time

No project goes 100% according to plan, so expect that developers will come across some problems that stump them for a day, will be off sick, or get called to work on an urgent bug on another system. Plan to lose some time.

Stop trimming testing time

Typically, on an ever tightening deadline, the testing phase is the one to get squeezed. If this happens a lot where you are, try padding it more in the first place.

Support your developers

It is no good 'letting' them order pizza – buy it for them. They are committing a lot of their own time to the project, you should at least treat them to food. Also, do not abandon them. It is not their fault that the project is late, so when they stay late to help out, you should be there with them, showing your support.

Bug fix and re-testing

I've seen many project plans with an amount of time for testing allocated at the end, and yet none for fixing the bugs found and re-testing the result. Things rarely work 100% first time.

Users hate testing

Testing is not a fun job for most, and users are often reticent to commit time to this important task. Get them to test early and often.

The following chapters dig deeper into these and other principles, which should help everyone involved to create better software products more effectively.

16

1. The Client

This section is intended to be read by the client of the software being developed - that is, the end user of the product. However, this section should be read by everyone involved.

Note that the client is not always the customer (that is to say, the end user) of the product. For example, the owner of a dating website may pay an agency to develop the website for him (making him the client), but it will be the public who actually use it on day to day basis. In these cases, it is important that the client also seeks the input of several customers in the development cycle.

For the sake of simplification, the 'client' is presumed here to be both the purchaser and the user of the software, and it is up to the reader to identify the person or persons most appropriate to fulfil the client's duties.

1.1 Be prepared to work for it

A successful project requires a **lot** of input from the client. Many clients naively produce a basic (and usually incomplete) specification and expect to receive a fully working system in return. Many clients (especially those that are external to the development company) are not experienced in producing such complex, detailed documents. They need to work closely with the business analysts/developers in the first instance to make sure that the specification is complete and then throughout the project to assist with any questions or missing details.

Furthermore, the client should be engaging in testing prototypes, new modules or iterative features as often as possible. In short, the client needs to devote substantial time to the project during its lifetime in order to improve its chances of success.

1.2 Cost vs time vs features – you choose

Here is the classic 'Iron Triangle' or Project Management Triangle.

The idea is to suggest that a project cannot have all of these attributes, it must be biased towards cost, or scope (features), or time (or quality). Sometimes this is reduced to fast (to develop), cheap (cost) and good (quality), with the idea being to ask the client to 'choose two', namely that they cannot have all three - one element will suffer at the focus of the others.

However, for small and medium business projects, I find this largely irrelevant. Clients will always want their product as cheaply as possible and as high quality as possible.

This basically reduces the discussion to cost versus features. The developer will naturally determine how to structure the internal workings of your project in order to meet the 'cheap yet as high quality as possible' criteria. As a client, you should concentrate on describing all of the features you need, then discuss pricing for those (preferably with different price points for different sub-sets of those features). Once you have (or are close to) agreeing the requirements and pricing, you can then ask if anything more can be done 'under the hood' to reduce cost. But bear in mind, if you try to squeeze the price too much, the developers might cut corners to meet it, and your product quality may well suffer. Concentrate on features versus cost.

1.3 Your costs **<u>will</u>** increase

It is a sad fact that many projects will run over-budget. Just as builders sometimes struggle to estimate the costs of housing projects, the same happens with software projects. Remember that the development staff are trying to automatically balance your project cost against a suitable level of quality. This does not leave much room for unseen problems (which occur often). If they "pad" the price too much, a client will not accept it. Depending on the size and complexity of your project, you should budget an extra 10-25% as contingency. Remember that usually, project overrun is a result of the client wishing to add more features, or having not scoped the initial requirements well enough.

Working to an agile development plan can help eliminate cost over-run, but that is still subject to having a good overall plan and specification from the start. Principle 1.19 - Consider iterative development – offers one possible solution to this problem.

1.4 Define requirements fully

Make sure you define your requirements as fully as possible. For example, if your project is a hotel booking system, there might be several modules required: client sign up, client profile editing, editing hotel availability data, hotel reservations and payments, booking adjustments and cancellations, emailing, reporting, and background and scheduled tasks.

For each of these sections you will need to think of all the operations that can be performed, what prerequisites, restrictions, rules or logic control and affect each operation, and the outcome of each operation (i.e. what will be affected and how, as a result of each action being performed).

It is a good idea to sit down with the developer (/analyst) and go over this document, even better to write it together. The developer will likely have more experience in requirements gathering than a client and will be able to ask probing questions to fill in any gaps, clarify assumptions made and improve poorly detailed logic. A poor specifications document will lead to poor estimates (or even worse, poor solution design), which can cost a lot of time the further into the project you get. Traditional wisdom says it is five times harder to fix if errors are not detected until the design stage, ten times harder not detected until coding, and 20 times if detected at the testing stage.

You may be asking yourself "If I use iterative/agile development, do I still need a specifications document?" The answer is yes, because without one, the overall system design often fails to capture some system logic or requirement, and it becomes difficult to add new features. I have seen this multiple times on agile projects that didn't create such a document first.

1.5 Define requirements consistently

Make sure you use consistent, every day natural language in your specification. It should be readable and (mostly) understandable by anyone. Also, ensure that any jargon is consistent (for example, if you have the notion of a 'season ticket' in your system, make sure it is always referred to as a 'season ticket' and by no other name. You should also structure your sentences for consistent layout. This will make your document easier to read and understand.

For example, look at these two definitions:

Account balances under 1,000 are considered low. Medium ranges from 1,000 to 10,000. The account is considered high when the amount exceeds 10,000.

Account balance is defined as follows:

low = under 1,000

medium = 1,000 to 10,000

high = over 10,000

The first block needs to be read carefully to interpret and understand it. Mixing of sentence structure also makes information absorption slower. The second block can be read and understood within two seconds or so. Being concise and to the point and consistently structured makes text quicker and easier to digest.

1.6 Include a glossary of terms

Where a project uses industry-specific jargon, include a glossary within the specifications document to explain them. Do not include such definitions within the main body of text. Once this jargon is understood, such explanations will only pollute the readability of the main body of the specification.

1.7 Simplify the requirements

Having decided to take the step into developing a bespoke software product, clients will frequently throw every conceivable feature into the mix with the idea that 'we are paying for it, may as well get everything we want'. However, remember that software is very expensive to develop. Do you really need all of those features? Are you over-engineering what it will do? By all means, envisage all the things that may be useful, but from that try to reduce your product's complexity down to only what is really needed. The result will be a better-produced system that is closer to your anticipated price and delivery date.

Further to this is the fact that (for waterfall development projects, where the entire software is scoped out beforehand), around 30% of functionality goes unused.

For Agile projects, it is good to envisage all the features you believe you need, but then only define the requirements for the most urgent or core parts of the system. Many of your other features may (and usually do) change as the system starts to take shape.

1.8 Prioritise requirements

Once you have come up with a list of requirements for your new system, make sure you list them in order of priority. You may want to label each feature or function as 'pre-requisite', 'desirable', and 'nice to have'. Another way to label them is with a notion of 'business value' that they provide (on a scale of 1-5, say). You can then discuss the price of each of these features with the project management, to see whether the price/value ratio makes them a high or medium priority for development, left until last 'if there is sufficient money and time', or cut from development altogether.

1.9 Consider iterative development

Typically for business software, an iterative approach works very well, especially with clients who are not used to defining their own software requirements. However it is those types of clients who typically shy away from iterative development in favour of the more traditional 'waterfall' method.

In the waterfall method, a specification is produced that details everything the system will do. A price and timetable will be agreed, then the developers go away and return with a finished product. Clients feel comfortable with this because they know what they will be getting and what it will cost, up front. However, unless they are well versed in defining software requirements, the result is often not fully effective. For example, systems developed in this method often end up with around 30% of their features never being used (wasting money), and having subsequent features being added on (even during development).

When a client receives a software product (complete or otherwise), they will often think of new features or ways for it to work, which are spurred on from having actual hands-on use. Being able to get their hands on the product early in the development cycle, allows the client to test their assumptions and design, and to steer subsequent feature development based on actual experience and use of the product. This is the crux of iterative development. The downside is that there is no 'complete specification' and hence no known, fixed price. This is scary to clients, especially those who are external to the development company. But designing how an entire system will work purely conceptually is difficult, even for experienced people. Getting hands on a work in progress provides a lot of insight and drives the imagination for the product's direction. Another downside to iterative development is that a new feature request may come along that will prove difficult to implement, as it may be incompatible with the system's design thus far.

One solution is to mix the two methodologies. This can be

done in one of two ways that I have found effective. The first, is to develop an absolute minimal system as a fixed cost, waterfall project, then move to iterative development to build it up with features as the client gets more and more hands-on time with the product. The second (more favourable) is to specify the entire system as one would for a waterfall project (including cost estimation), but then prioritise and work on the features in an iterative manner. This should give the client a good idea of the final cost (allowing them to assign a budget), and allow them to dictate new features based on cost and usefulness as the product develops. The benefits of this hybrid system mean that clients have a sense of budget control over the development as a whole, but can also dictate which features are more valuable and should be included, to maximise product usefulness versus cost. It also drastically reduces the 'feature waste' that occurs on projects using the waterfall method, whilst giving the developers a good idea of all the functional requirements that may be requested in the near future.

1.10 Avoid exceptions in requirements

Consider this requirement:

"There will be three levels of membership: Bronze, Silver and Gold. Gold members can also be given Executive status."

Depending on what you want to do with the "executive" status, it may be better to have four levels of membership: Bronze, Silver, Gold and Gold Executive.

Look at what options or features this "executive" option will control and consider implementing it both ways as described above. Generally, the less "if" conditions exist in your system's logic design, the more consistent the processing is, the easier to use, quicker to build, and quite possibly less error prone your resulting system will be.

1.11 Avoid solutions in requirements

Requirements should specify *what* is needed, but now *how* it is implemented. Consider the following two requirements statements:

1. The user should be able to select the support level from a drop-down combo box.

2. The user should be able to select the support level easily.

In this is a somewhat oversimplified example, the first statement is offering a solution, that is, to use a drop-down combo box. The second is leaving the implementation details to the UI/UX/development team. Unless you have very specific needs on *how* something is implemented (this should be very rare), restrict your requirements to only *what* is needed.

1.12 Define required availability

It is not enough to specify what the system should do – you also need to specify how often it can do it. For example, is the software going to be used internally in an office, only during office hours? Is it going to be a website that is used globally and needs to be available 99.99% of the time?

Many client/server projects (e.g. websites, or phone apps that connect to a central database) often run on a single server. On average such servers manage around 99.8% uptime (e.g. approximately 1 day per year of outage). If you need more uptime (availability), then put the details in the specifications document. The cost for providing 3, 4 or 5 "nines" of uptime (that is 99.9%, 99.99% or 99.999%) raises considerably, and may not be financially viable.

1.13 Define disaster recovery times

An important factor of your uptime requirements is the disaster recovery time. A system that is up for 99.8% of the time may only be unavailable for a 20 minutes each week. However, it is more likely to be fine for 2 years and then face a hardware failure, taking 2 days to fix. Can you afford that? In the case of a server failure, data loss, etc., how much continual time can your system be unavailable for? If all your data is lost, how fresh does your data back-up need to be? Can you afford to lose one day of data? One hour?

Maybe you can afford to lose 1 day of data, but you want your system back online within 2-3 hours during normal office hours. Again, the quicker you want to be able to recover from disaster and the less data you are prepared to lose, the higher the cost will be (and these costs rise disproportionally) . Generally these costs are on the hardware/platform side, but considerations may have to be made in the software product design to meet your uptime and recovery time requirements. These variables should be defined in your Business Continuity Planning. Whatever your needs are, document them.

1.14 Define server load and response times

How many users will be using your system concurrently? How quickly should the system respond? How much data will it hold? These questions will affect not only your physical server set-up but maybe the software design as well, so make sure they are documented. For example, you may state "the system will respond to 95% of requests within 3 seconds, given 100 concurrent users and 1 million documents in the database". It is unwise to expect 100% of requests to be processed within a specific time, but you may want to specify a time-out, e.g. "any requests taking longer than 15 seconds will display a 'system busy' message".

1.15 Anticipate growth and capacity planning

You should also describe the anticipated rate of growth of usage of your software product. Will the number of active users increase 10% per year? Will the number of historical transaction records increase by 1 million each year? Make sure some estimates are included in your document, to enable the system designers (and hardware implementers) to cater for your future needs.

1.16 Define hardware requirements

Does your software have to run on an existing server or platform? Does it need to share resources with other software? Does it need to run on the web browsers of 98% of the active net population today? Maybe it is designed to run on a desktop Operating System – if so which versions?

These requirements should be clearly documented in your specifications.

1.17 Engage the development team often

Make sure you are on hand to respond to requests for information or more detail from developers. You should also encourage iterative development so that you can see and test progress as it is made with each release cycle.

Many projects are delayed because clients do not make themselves available to answer questions from their software developers. It is not enough to drop off a specification document then sit back and wait for the product to be delivered. You will need to commit at least a few hours a week during development. The more responsive you are, the quicker and better your product will be produced.

Note that this does not mean you should be calling them up, asking for progress reports, or worse yet, asking for features to be added or changed. These type of questions and requests need to go through the project management and a defined change management process.

2. The Analyst/Programmer

This section is intended to be read by those performing the requirements analysis and actual development of the software in question, though everyone would derive some benefit from this section.

Note that some companies may employ an analyst/developer to perform this role, whereas others might split this into two separate roles: a business analyst and a developer.

Personally, I am not a fan of the latter. Separating out the role of analysis and design/development means there is a knowledge gap between the two. If you have an analyst/programmer who designs the system and is involved day to day with its creation, and who is also performing the analysis role, the result is someone who has an intimate knowledge of the user requirements and how they are implemented, which I consider very important for a successful project. This is especially important for iterative for subsequent development phases, where the analyst can steer the client to be consistent with existing design, or warn of new requirements that will clash with current implementation details.

2.1 Gather requirements fully

Poor requirements specifications are the main reason for problems and delays in projects. If possible work directly with your client to produce this document (visit their premises if an external client) and take some time to understand how their business works. Also make sure every section, subsection, and paragraph are numbered, it makes for easier referencing when talking about the document in subsequent discussions.

In recent years there has been a tendency to steer away from the waterfall project method (which required a full specifications document upfront, then delivered a final product at the end, that matched the specifications), and instead follow the agile methodologies currently enjoying the limelight, which do not call for a specifications document but instead develop small parts of functionality in small cycles, feeding these back to the customer for further guidance on what features to develop next.

This is fine if you are a multinational software development company (such as Apple) who develop their own software, have huge stable teams and have been doing this for years (even then, Apple have dumped and re-written their OS's from scratch a few times over). But for most small and medium business, and especially those with external clients, this lack of specifications causes weaknesses in design and problems later on.

Forcing the client to produce a specifications document really focuses them to think in detail about their requirements, and also provides an analyst a perfect opportunity to steer the client away from weak software design decisions. Once this document has been produced, the software can still be developed using agile processes, only now there will be a bedrock of understanding.

2.2 Understand your clients' priorities

It's a simple fact that system requirements will likely change whilst you are still working on the system. It is important that you try to understand as much as possible about your client's needs, so you can help direct them when they ask for new features or changes. Tell them how much extra work/cost is involved for their changes, advise them if you feel the cost/benefit ratio is not in their favour. You can only really do this if you spend some time to get to know your client, and understand what is really important to their business.

2.3 Maintain conceptual integrity

Conceptual errors are significantly more expensive than syntax errors when it comes to correcting a system. Syntax errors are typically restricted to the module they are contained within, whereas conceptual errors typically span many code modules.

Firstly, make sure all entities that are created are named consistently. For example, if you have a flight number as an attribute, make sure it is called the same in the specifications document, system code, and database. Do not call it flightNum in the database and flightId elsewhere, for instance. Ideally, you would use variable names that support self-documenting code (i.e. names that sufficiently describe the data they hold).

Secondly, ensure that error handling routines, data structures and component calling/messaging structures are as consistent as possible between all code modules.

Also ensure that all entities (e.g. objects, modules) created aim for the lowest coupling and highest cohesion possible (see section 2.4).

2.4 Low coupling, high cohesion

When designing a system (or a collection of modules), you should aim for low coupling and high cohesion between those modules.

Coupling refers to the amount of dependency one module has on another. For example, with highly (or tightly) coupled modules, changes in one will cause a 'ripple effect' of changes on dependent modules. Such an example would be modules sharing some global data. Changes in the structure to that global data will affect all modules using it. Low (or loosely) coupled modules communicate through a narrow interface (such as passing fixed parameters or messages), such that inner changes to one module should not affect dependent modules.

Cohesion is a measure of how strongly-related the individual functions of a module are with respect to each other. The more "cohesive" a module is, the more related and consistent its functions are, which is more desirable. An example of low cohesion would be functions that have been grouped together because they occur sequentially in a processing order (even though the functions may operate on different domains), or grouped together because they form a "logical" group, even though the inputs and outputs of the functions will vary considerably (such as grouping all video and sound functions together in an "output handler" module). High cohesion occurs when all the functions in a module carry out a small number of related tasks: for example, a module that generates PDF files.

Higher cohesion creates a more maintainable system, as changes in one module should not impact other modules as much (if at all), plus those modules will be of reduced complexity, affording easier understanding.

2.5 Design for change

It is safe (and wise) to assume that the requirements will change, even while you are still developing. By keeping your design as modular, loosely coupled and as cohesive as possible, you make it easier to change the system, both for now and future requirements changes or additions.

However, this needs to be balanced against making any particular module or unit too generic (or too configurable). If, when making a module generic or extensible, it complicates the structure and understanding significantly, then you might have a conceptual design issue.

On the other hand, if the generic/extensible changes simplify your module structure (say, for example, you have implemented a factory method that can return object types which you can later extend), then you have a good conceptual design.

2.6 Design and code for efficiency

Be wary of execution time and memory footprint of your code, especially with respect to the availability and concurrency requirements. For example, on a client-server system, if you need to read through many records in a database (performing processing one record at a time), do not use functions that cache all the records in to memory first. There should be other, non-caching functions available. Such caching can make your script consume hundreds of megabytes of memory, and if you multiply that by your expected user concurrency figures, you may easily run out of server memory.

The same goes for execution time. Divide your expected user concurrency by an average time between operations to calculate script concurrency (e.g. 300 users performing one action every 30 seconds = 10). If a script needs to have 10 instances running concurrently, you really need to make sure it executes in under 1/10th of a second (assuming only one server is running the system). For the odd script it may be OK to overrun, but keep an eye on the performance **while** you are developing. Memory and execution profiling tools exist for most languages and systems. Make use of them.

2.7 Design for now, not the future

It is very tempting, when developing a code module, to add features that might be needed in the future. Do not add any features which will not be needed in the next 6-12 months. The chances are the requirements will change before then, and you would have wasted development time. Wait until the need is a certainty.

On the other hand, if you are aware that certain other features will be (or very likely be) required, but you do not need to implement them now, then make provisions/considerations for them in your current code design. This is where a detailed system specification comes in handy, even during iterative development.

2.8 Be careful of generality

Another temptation is to make a module as flexible as possible so that it can be re-used. However, unless you have a specific need to re-use this component in the immediate future, the chances are your time will be wasted. Add to this the fact that generalisation often makes a component slower.

It is often better to design your component for the immediate requirements, but structure it and add comments to make it easier to extend and generalise if needed in the future.

2.9 Consider design alternatives

Test assumptions about the speed, memory or system requirements of one solution versus another. Do not always settle for the first solution you come up with. If you have a couple of ways to design something but do not actually know which is best, try prototyping both methods to test them. This should not happen too often, but when it does, the additional module development time spent on this will typically pay off later.

2.10 Build in software safety

Programming code will always contain errors and weak points. Always add error/bounds checking code. Do not assume that all input values will be within expected or allowed ranges. If you use a case statement, always add a 'default' catch. Make sure you check the responses to all module, object and database functions for errors and trap/report them as required.

With internet accessible systems, safety also implies security. If processing user input (or machine input from another domain), assume it will be 'dirty' (e.g. contain SQL or script injections, buffer overflow attempts, etc.) and clean/validate it accordingly.

2.11 Avoid exceptions in design

There will likely always be a few special cases in a system that need to be coded and handled differently. However, if too many logical exceptions appear, you are likely working with a bad design. That could either be a bad design of a well-specified system (in which case the design needs changing) or a bad design due to a bad requirements specification. In the latter case, you need to correct the specification as soon as possible and calculate any additional cost or delay incurred.

2.12 Design and code for maintainability

This should be one of the most critical goals of software design and coding. In the first instance, making your code and design easy to read and comprehend will also likely make it immediately less buggy.

Avoid coding tricks. Make code easy to read (left to right and top-down). Do not nest more than six levels deep. Follow coding standards. Write self-documenting code and fewer comments.

Here is a typical line of code:

```
for($i=0; $i<$j; $i++)   /* loop through all the pages */
```

and here is a self-documenting version:

```
for($thisPage=0; $thisPage<$pageCount; $thisPage++)
```

There is no need for a separate comment, the variable and function/method names document what is happening.

Comments should not be included line by line, describing what each line is doing, but should relate to a block of 10 to 30 lines, and describe the higher level function which that block of code is performing – and why.

2.13 Write comments before code

It is a very useful technique to start coding a module with just high-level comments. This ensures you have thought about the structure and is a perfect representation of the requirements. Not only does it make it easier to code (filling in the gaps), it serves as a check that you have understood the requirements properly. If you have to change the comments, then your solution design or understanding of the requirements was initially incorrect.

2.14 Tune for performance later

When coding a module that has complex performance issues, get it working first. Projects are often under a lot of time constraints, so you are better off making sure it is working within the required time-scale. Your client will more likely appreciate a system that is complete, but slow and can be tuned, to an incomplete or late system.

2.15 Avoid context switching

Where possible you should avoid working on more than one system or module at a time. Multitasking (specifically, switching from one project to another in this case) requires you to 'recall' all of the details of the second project. This is known as a context switch and is very expensive time-wise.

When a developer is in full flow on a system, he or she will have hundreds of things in their memory: variable and function names; their parameters; database layout; directory and file names of source code elements and so forth. All of this knowledge is held in short term, quick-access memory - go on holiday for two weeks and all of it would have gone, and will probably take several days to come back. Likewise, switching to another project requires you to re-remember these details from the second project, which, depending on the size of the second project and your task, can take a very long time, reducing productivity to as little as 20%.

Developers switching between multiple tasks is one of the greatest unrealised time killers. You should structure your work to avoid this as much as possible.

2.16 Use version control

All source code (and supporting files such as graphics, documents, etc) should be stored in a modern version control system. Do not comment out old code – remove it. Make sure programmers have their own logins to version control and that all commits are documented and logged against the person responsible. Branches should be used to store different release versions.

2.17 Mentally execute your code

After coding a module (or any naturally self-contained block of code), run through the code and execute it in your mind. This is a simple and inexpensive way to debug your code early on.

2.18 Write software to be 'just good enough'

Sometimes code modules can be 'over-engineered' to provide extra functionality that might one day be useful, but is not actually needed now. Such code usually ends up unused. Instead, write the function or module in question once, and make it 'just good enough' that it satisfies the current specifications and immediate short term requirements, and does not need to be revisited. Any enhancements to this module are part of a separate project, with its own time-scale and budget.

2.19 Hacked code is rarely revisited

Too often, code is 'hacked in' as a temporary measure (be it laziness or cutting corners to save time, or dodging a complex programming issue), with the intention of 're-doing it properly' later. But time constraints and other projects often prevent this from ever happening. If the project timetable afforded you ten hours to develop this module, but you are behind and know you can 'hack it' in two, this actually worse. You will still have to do it properly later, meaning about ten hours of work later. When a project is behind, do not do in twelve hours what you can do once, properly, in ten. Do not leave hacked code in place, it is deficient in some way: otherwise it could not have been done so quickly.

2.20 Build throwaway prototypes

Sometimes there is a particular problem that is difficult to solve or the requirements are vague. In such cases you can build a prototype to demonstrate and test the theory of the design that has been provided or created. In these cases it should be developed as quickly as possible, using any language and tools that you fancy (i.e. that allow you to complete it the quickest). This is where 'quick and dirty' wins. The objective is purely to test that your hypothesis, the design, algorithm, UI or whatever it is, does in fact work as expected. You can then throw the prototype away and code it properly.

2.21 Give prototypes to clients early

In some cases, the prototype in question is to check or validate something that the client has stated or assumed, or to show them how, for example, a particular user interface might work. In such cases, where it is the client who needs to validate the prototype, get it to them as early as possible. Changes to the specifications might arise as a result, and you want to discover them as early as possible in the development cycle.

2.22 Document your assumptions

An assumption made during coding or system design typically means an oversight in the specifications document, so make sure that assumptions are documented and are fed back to the client and into the specifications document, as required, and as soon as possible. Remember, any changes to the specifications document should trigger a re-evaluation of the development schedule.

2.23 Leverage open source software

These days, there is an abundance of open source software available, covering every typical computing function. Whether it is a language compiler or interpreter, a web, file, database or email server, development environments and frameworks, testing, deployment or monitoring tools, or a replacement for general office software, just about everything has an open source solution available, and you would be wise to leverage as much of this as possible.

In the 1970's it was typical for developers to create their own libraries of useful code, and to take them from job to job to save development time. Then, in the 1980's and 1990's, commercial software companies saw software as their commercial advantage and kept all source code as their own. Indeed, join a development company today and your contract will most likely state that any and all code you develop belongs to them alone. We have since come full-circle, and open source software and libraries have become widespread throughout the development community. Open-source products continue to replace commercial equivalents throughout the computing world. Commercial companies even pay staff to work on open source software and contribute their developments back to the projects freely.

Besides the (zero) cost of ownership, open source software benefits from the masses continually contributing, fixing and improving it, meaning you can find mature, stable and tested libraries, tools or products right across the software spectrum. Make the most of this wherever you can.

2.24 Understand low level code

Do not rely completely on libraries and frameworks to provide all of the functionality you need. It is important to know how to hand-code various solutions as well.

I have seen several programmers who are not able to solve typical programming problems themselves and instead rely virtually exclusively on frameworks, libraries, and public domain code to piece together their solutions.

One such example was that of a code library that a programmer used to handle the unzipping of files. This library was very large and offered numerous unneeded features, whereas the language in question had an unzip feature built in, requiring only a few lines of code to operate.

Such poor use of a library makes the application in question a lot slower and more memory hungry, more difficult and cumbersome to understand and install, and does nothing to improve the programmer's 'knowledge toolbox'.

2.25 Use the most appropriate tools

Do not use a new library or framework just because you have discovered it. Whilst most programmers are keen (and should be encouraged) to learn about new technologies, weigh up their use in a commercial system carefully. For example, the introduction of a new technology or tool may affect the following areas:

- Learning curve for other developers.
- Larger application (more memory intensive).
- Additional cost or knowledge for support roles.
- Incompatibilities with other software and/or versions.
- Incompatibilities with the development, test or live server environments.
- Complicate a server's patching or upgrade path.
- Less performant.
- Licensing costs or collisions with existing software.
- Regression testing.

Consider these points carefully before deciding to use a new tool, library or framework. Do not use it just because it looks good on your C.V.

2.26 Think hard, code easy

Given a task that should take 10 hours, good programmers will think about it for 2 hours and complete it maybe in a further five. Average programmers will just start and do it in 10 hours.

Programmers sometimes tend to solve a coding problem (designing the solution or even specifying functional behaviour) whilst they are coding. If done correctly, a programmer will think carefully for a while without coding anything. He will mentally try out different solutions in his mind, until the most appropriate one materialises. Once 'chosen', the programmer will find the resulting code just flowing out into the keyboard. Such code is also typically more consistent and structured.

2.27 If it isn't broken, don't fix it

There is often a temptation to fix code that looks bad or is written poorly and to clean it up. If it is a simple case of presentation (spacing, indentation etc.) then that is OK, but changing live code that is working fine can introduce new bugs – do not risk it. If it is really bothering you, then plan some time to fix it properly.

2.28 Code deteriorates over time

The older a piece of code is, the more likely that "hacks" or "band-aids" have been used to patch it up and extend it. In addition, it may end up having its functionality extended beyond the limits of its original design, creating sub-standard code. Eventually, it will reach the point where it is cheaper to tear it down and re-build it from the ground up. Working with a poor, difficult code base is one of the major reasons for developers changing companies (and a regular contributor to project lateness). It can cause an unhappy working environment. Try to keep your environment happy by avoiding hacks and quick fixes where possible. The cleaner you can keep your work, the more enjoyable it will be to keep working on it.

2.29 Take responsibility

Further to 2.28 above, if it is you that has added quick hacks and bad code to a system, then it will be you who becomes increasingly unhappy working on it and eventually looking for a new job.

If you have had to implement some poor quality code in order to meet a deadline, for example, tell your project manager about it, so you can arrange some time to fix it later.

Be pragmatic about your work: write code that you are proud of, take responsibility for what you create, admit when you have made mistakes or faltered, and try to develop the right thing as often as possible. The more pride you have in the work you produce every day, the longer you will be happy in your job.

2.30 Take pride in your work

Programming is a creative art. There are countless ways to code a solution to a problem, some better than others. Take pride in coding the most elegant, maintainable, and simplistic solution you can each time, within the constraints given. If you can look back on most days and say 'I'm proud of the code I produced today', then you are probably doing the best job you can. Lack of pride often translates to poor quality code.

3. Testing

Testing is very much treated as the runt of the litter when it comes to resources on a project. It is very expensive to perform, and because frequently managers see no instant benefit from it, it becomes viewed as a 'nice to have', or is originally allocated time but then subsequently squeezed as the project begins to creep over its original time scales.

However testing is a crucial part of the software development process, and whilst you may find you do not have the luxury of time to write and perform all of the testing you might desire, even a little bit of the right testing in the right place can go a long way towards improving the quality of your software product.

3.1 Walk through bugs with other developers

If you get stuck on a particular programming problem, it is often very helpful to ask another programmer to take a look at it with you. Walk and talk them through the piece of code in question line by line. Often, you will end up paying more attention to the code yourself as you try explain it to someone else, and will spot the problem yourself. And if you don't spot it, usually the fresh pair of eyes will.

3.2 Write your own test plans and test code

Contrary to the general idea that a programmer should never write their own test code or test plans, in the modern business software world it is OK, as the alternative seems to be that little or no structured testing is done at all. If your company has enough developers that different people can be assigned to testing, then great. In my experience though, this has been less than 10% of cases. Coupled with the end users not investing sufficient time in testing, and it is clear that anything you can do to provide more testing can only be a good thing. Writing your own test code is far better than having none at all.

3.3 Write automated tests

Automated tests (both unit and system-wide, plus any other scripts that you can write to test something) are invaluable. Write as many tests as you can within the time available, and mix up test types. Any pain you feel writing them will be outweighed significantly by the benefits you will feel afterwards, especially when you can regression test after subsequent feature development.

Even a basic set of automated smoke tests (i.e. a non-exhaustive set of tests that check for basic functionality) will make deployments and new code integrations easier, providing you with some assurance that you are not about to 'break something'.

3.4 Written Test plans still have usefulness

Before the year 2000, very little was available in terms of open source testing tools. As a result, automated testing didn't really exist in many small companies, and manual 'test plans' were created. These would often be a list of actions for a user to perform and check responses against.

These days testing should be automated as much as possible, so that it can be executed at high speed and repeated at will. However, there is still a use for creating a manual 'test plan'.

There is no need to document every operation and key-press or response needed, but take the time to list functions and operations that are likely to break or are more critical (for example, on a website service, you might list logging in, creating an account, purchasing membership options, and so forth). Use this document as a "general overview" for tests that you subsequently automate. It will be a handy reference for identifying tests you have created so far, and as a reference for non-developers to understand what your testing covers. Remember, tests create confidence in a system, but that confidence is hard to share with non-technical staff. When nearing a release date, management may ask you something like "does the testing cover membership payments? We cannot afford for that to go wrong", to which you will be able to reply "yes – here is a list of the tests that we automate for each release". Such a document will create peace of mind for you as well.

3.5 Black box testing

Black box testing refers to testing a module without knowledge of its inner workings, treating it as a "black box". The only reference to what it should do and how, are gained from reading the specifications document and the module documentation, without referring to any of its code.

The documentation should specify all the inputs, operations, and expected outputs that the module supports. From this, you can test each of its functions, including throwing random, invalid and incomplete inputs at the module.

3.6 White box testing

White box testing, by contrast, involves exploiting knowledge of a module's internal code structure. For example, if you know that a particular parameter should be an integer with a range from 1 to 10 inclusive, test all the edge cases for that variable (0, 1, 2, 9, 10, 11) as well as some out of bounds values (-1, 0.9, ABC, 23467823, etc.)

It might also be, for example, that certain inputs within a certain range, cause additional code to be executed. Without internal knowledge like this, you may miss testing parts of the functionality.

A code coverage report (see 3.9) will also (and more accurately) identify whether or not your tests have covered such conditional code.

3.7 Unit and System tests

Much emphasis is placed on unit tests only, but I would also suggest writing automated system tests. For example, if your system provides an API to say, a user authentication database, then write automated tests that invoke the API endpoints, and create a test database for it to work against. This will test all of the code, end to end, and may also catch bugs in the interface code between modules, particularly if low cohesion exists.

A traditional approach would be to write unit tests for each module and 'mock' (or 'stub') the interface calls made from that module to others, to make sure you are testing only the module in question. However, I find it more time (hence cost) effective to consider 'system tests' where you can switch (for example) the database layer to a test database, and write extra code to clear and reset the test data at will, rather than spend time mocking interfaces. Mocked interfaces can take quite a lot of time to code (unit tests typically take just as long to develop as the code they are testing) and worse still, they often stagnate towards uselessness as the module evolves, but developers fail to updates the tests. However, adding a small amount of code to switch targets (such as a live/test database) and testing the modules how they would actually interact within a system context, can yield significant time savings. No one way is universally better than the other – use whichever is most appropriate for your modules and system in question.

3.8 Regression testing

Changes made after an initial release (maintenance and enhancements) can cause more bugs than the original development phase. It is therefore important to be able to regression test as much as possible, preferably through automated testing. Automated test code can be expensive to create, but testing at least some core or delicate modules can help bolster system integrity significantly. It is here especially, that automated system tests pay off. And remember, *some* tests are better than none, as long as they are testing something of use.

3.9 Code coverage reports

One enormous benefit of the unit testing frameworks available is that of code coverage reports. It is easy to see at a glance, how many of the logic paths through a particular code module have been covered by your test suite. This information, together with white box unit tests, can help you very quickly determine any sensitive or potentially problematic areas of code that still need tests written for them.

Aiming for 100% code coverage is very time consuming, and not usually required. Most companies seem to aim for 80% code coverage in any one module (which means both 80% of each function, and 80% of the number of functions). If you can achieve more without significant time investment, then great. If you cannot get to 80% though, make sure you spend your time developing tests of use. There is little value, for example, in writing unit tests for all of the non-essential reporting modules, whilst ignoring the main "interest amortization calculation" module. Do what is needed the most, not what is easiest. Quality over quantity is the key for unit tests.

4. Project Management

This section is aimed at those managing software projects. However, development and testing staff would also benefit from this section.

4.1 Software Configuration Management

One of the most crucial jobs for a project manager is setting up a suitable SCM system/process. In essence, your SCM should help you manage:

- Ensuring adherence to development processes
- Processes and tools used in builds
- The software and hardware platforms needed to host your product
- Configuration details for hardware, software, and virtual environments.
- Interactions between team members
- Interactions between stakeholders and developers
- Defect tracking
- Change control: feature requests and requirements
- Version release control

You can use a mixture of software and/or paper processes to manage this, however you see fit. But make sure these processes are documented and adhered to, in order to ensure a smoother project life-cycle.

4.2 Use light processes

With all the tracking and processes listed in 4.1 above, it is quite easy to implement a large system that covers everything off-the-shelf. However, do not get bogged down in record keeping and long-winded processes. Make sure that whichever system you use, that you capture only what you need and with the minimum of interruption to actual daily work.

Too many companies obtain some software or SaaS product that provides these tracking and management tools, then they try to use too many features of said product. Make sure you start off small, introducing practices and processes for the most critical paths first. Keep all processes as light as possible. These tools are supposed to assist in the tracking of your progress, not detract from it.

Email should **not** be at the centre of your processes. Email is essentially random data pieces that have been date-stamped. Email is not structured enough to provide a quick overview and update information on projects. Email should be used as an exception to your daily routine, not as a routine part of it. You would be far better off using any of the open source free project management tools available.

4.3 Use version numbers, not names

Which Ubuntu version came first - Vivid Vervet or Wily Werewolf? Which OS X operating system version came first - Mavericks or Mountain Lion? For Android OS, in which order were Marshmallow, Jelly Bean and KitKat released? And what does that tell me about the product?

Whilst such names might be great for marketing etc. (which is doubtful in itself), internally you should always refer to project versions by sequential numbers. It just makes life so much easier. These version numbers should also be stored/reflected in your source control system.

4.4 Use your best analyst

Requirements specifications are key to a successful project. Whenever possible, use your best analyst/programmer for requirements gathering (in conjunction with the client as much as possible) and systems design. Allow less experienced analysts to learn from them by shadowing them, then ease them into module and systems design gradually.

4.5 Keep clients and developers apart

Whilst it is encouraged to ask your analyst/programmer to help your client with the systems specification, after this step, all inbound communication should go through the project manager and/or the analyst. It is all too common for clients to ask developers directly for changes and additions to their project (especially where the client and developer work in the same company), and for developers to want to accommodate them. However, such conversations and requests must go through proper change control procedures, and anything resulting in more development work must undergo impact analysis.

In the case of Agile development, which advocates continuous customer collaboration, note that this should only occur between sprints. During sprint time, developers should be left alone to work on the tasks allocated.

4.6 The ideal team size is two or three

When trying to work out who should work on what section of a project and in what teams, you should consider keeping your teams as small as possible. There are a few reasons for this:

- Combinatorial explosion of communications.
- Divisibility of tasks.
- Varied relative skill levels of developers.

The first point deals with the fact that, as additional members are added to a team, the amount of communications between them grows polynomially. With 2 people, there is only 1 line of communication, with 3 people, there are 3 lines of communication, and so on. With 6 people there are 15 possible lines of communication.

Obviously, people on a team need to talk to each other, to discuss what they are working on, how it interacts with the work of the others, etc. The amount of communication can be reduced by using smaller teams and have them working on isolated modules of a project. Modern practices such as iterative development help to achieve this naturally, subject to the second point being made: divisibility of tasks.

The more divisible a task is, the more likely you can have a small team working on it with minimal communication overhead with other teams. However, the division of the tasks is often incorrectly performed by the project manager, whereas it should be down to the analyst or respective developers, who will understand the intricacies of interactions within the system at large and will better understand where the points of lowest coupling can occur (see 2.4) for a better modular approach.

The final point refers to the relative skills of the developers in a team. With a team of four or more, you are likely to have a range of proficiency. The slower developers will impact the speed of the faster ones, as they ask for assistance, or simply do not complete their section of work as quickly. With a team of two or three this is much less of a problem, and less proficient developers can be put to work in smaller or less complicated sub-sections of the project.

So, to recap, one is the ideal team size in terms of communication overhead (as there is none), but two is better for bouncing ideas around and coming up with better solutions. A team of three introduces more communication overhead, but still improves the rate at which work can be completed. Team sizes from four upwards will yield ever decreasing benefit in completion time vs labour cost.

4.7 Use pair programming for complex logic

Pair programming is the practice of having two developers sit at one computer and write code. Normally there is one developer in the 'hot seat' and another observing. They may take it in turns to do the actual coding.

Pair programming is clearly expensive, but the cost is marginalised when used sparingly in certain circumstances. The first is when developing a complex piece of logic. The second set of eyes helps catch bugs as each line of code is written, plus both of them will interact and come up with more solutions and ideas when tackling complex obstacles. In these cases, the cost of pair programming is offset against the time spent debugging the resulting code.

Another use for pair programming is knowledge transfer. It is an ideal way to educate less experienced programmers, and is also ideal for new employees to help get up to speed on your code base and form friendships with their new colleagues.

4.8 Projects rarely finish, they evolve

Software systems are rarely developed, deployed and forgotten about in business. Usually, once a project has been deployed, further enhancements, functionality and bug fixes will continue to roll in. Bear this in mind with your projects. Often (especially towards the end of a project) there are temptations to cut corners to "get the job done". These will come back to bite you. Time saved by cutting corners will probably cost you several times more, further down the line.

4.9 Estimating project costs

Estimate all of the development tasks. If any task is greater than 1 day, split it in to sub-tasks and re-estimate those, continuing to divide any task which lasts longer than 1 day.

Sum the development days, then multiply this by 1.32 (this is because we assume developers work at 80% efficiency, and that every 10 days 1 day will be randomly lost). You now have a figure we will call development days.

All other figures are a multiple of development days.

- Test days will either be:
    - 20% of development days (minimal unit testing)
    - 35% of development days (comprehensive unit testing)
    - 50% of development days (if testing includes regression, complex, and/or cross-system testing)
- Analysis days will be 10% of development days.
- Project management days will be 5% of development days.

You can now multiply each of these days (development, test, analysis, management) against a suitable cost for each, to determine your project's overall development cost.

4.10 Estimating project time-scales

Break down system development into tasks and estimate each task. Any task that takes more than one day should be further sub-divided until all tasks take one day or less. You now have the number of 'man days' of development.

For the other work elements, assume that: full analysis and documentation will take 10% of development time; testing will take 20-50% of development time; management overhead (this includes project meetings) will take 2.5 - 10% of development time (aim for 2.5%-5%, which is one to two hours per week).

Deployment time is too project specific to provide guidelines, but if you have to rely on external departments or providers to complete work for you, allow 2-3 extra days.

Now you must determine development and testing resource concurrency. For example, if two developers are working on tasks from different modules and their task estimates add up to 50 hours each, then you can put 50 'elapsed' hours as the calendar estimate. However, if they are working within the same module, add 5% for two developers and 10% for three developers. This is to allow for communication overhead between them. So, 50 hours per person for two persons, becomes (100 * 105% / 2) = 52.5 elapsed hours. 50 hours per person for three persons becomes (150 * 110% / 3) = 55 hours. Once you work out which developers and testers are working on which tasks, you can determine the overall 'elapsed' time using the above formula, before adding on the analysis, management and deployment times.

Then you need to add an additional 'unplanned' day for every 10 elapsed days to reach your overall elapsed days count, before factoring in any known holidays or other reasons for resource unavailability, to arrive at your final calendar date estimate.

4.11 Delivery dates come from developers only

Do not let company requirements dictate delivery dates. If there is a fixed date that you wish to work to (for instance, an annual trade show that is a perfect product launching opportunity), then ask the developer to provide individual estimates for several pieces of work, but do not mention the deadline. From his response, you can see what can be done in time and what features you may need to trim. Any mention of a deadline to a developer whilst they are trying to calculate estimates, will likely influence them as they try to accommodate your wishes, to your eventual detriment.

4.12 Give your projects breathing space

Too often, one project is planned to start immediately after the previous one finishes, resulting in *all* future planned projects being late. Most projects finish late or run into problems, so schedule some 'breathing space' at the end. If a project is then on time, you will appreciate starting the next one early, or using this time for those 'would like to do' jobs that you never get time for. If your project overruns, you will appreciate this extra time without jeopardizing subsequent project dates.

4.13 Don't over-pad schedules

If a project falls a little behind schedule, staff will often 'chip in' to help get back on track. Never push this too far though, as it will cause resentment. Conversely, a task with a lot of padding will actually waste time. Your developers may well work slower if they think "it's OK, I have a week to do this task". It is a nice 'gift' to offer them from time to time, but don't over-pad a project as the staff will naturally slow down and use up that time – whether subconsciously or otherwise.

Think about it. If you were asked to be somewhere 1 mile (1.6km) away, in 15 minutes, you would walk pretty quickly, maybe even jog a little. But if you were asked to get there in 1 hour, you would walk slowly, casually. You might even stop for a coffee along the way. You are unlikely to rush there and arrive very early. So it is with development, especially when you are doing it day in day out. Allow your staff to get there at a comfortable pace, but do not allow them to go too slowly.

4.14 Expect something to go wrong

For every 10 calendar days of elapsed development time (irrespective of how many developers are working in parallel), insert an extra 'unplanned' day. This is not a day you should be expecting to charge the customer (although it should be factored into your own costs), it is for the myriad of things that can and typically do delay a project. This could be staff sickness, desktop or server failure, company-wide internet outage or power loss, emergencies from other projects, dealing with a cyber attack, etc.

Add this day to your project as a 'spare' day. Do not plan anything for it. When you come to that day in the plan, if you are still on track as you planned, great, continue to work as normal within your schedule (you should now be a day ahead). If you are still ahead when you finish the project, everyone will be happy. If not, you will be happy you added this extra buffer.

4.15 Remove developers from a late project

The normal reaction to a development task over-running is to want to add more staff to work on it. However, this rarely works, due to the time needed to bring someone else up to speed, the additional communication overhead, etc.

In actual fact, the opposite is often true. In a team of four or more programmers, you are likely to have at least one which is less capable. This person will actually slow down the faster, more capable developers with their questions, mistakes, etc. If that person is working with one or more others on a task that is proceeding too slowly, removing that person from the task may well speed it up. In such cases, you should assign them to a task which is more in keeping with their skill set. On a later task or project, you can re-unite them with the more capable staff with the view to encourage skills mentoring.

4.16 Keep updating plans and schedules

Things **will** change along the way, it is inevitable. Mistakes will be made, something would have been overlooked, or new ideas and features will be imagined and requested. Whenever the goal changes, do not just try to 'shoe-horn' it into your project. Make sure you calculate the time impact and update your project plan and schedule accordingly.

4.17 Measure and refine estimates

Estimating software development effort is non-trivial and varies from person to person and between different situations. It is therefore paramount, if you are continuously developing software, to refine your estimate methods and accuracy.

This needs to be done at an individual level, not team level. For example, if you are using sprint planning and scrum points estimation, then usually all your developers estimate the tasks individually and you take an average. But one developer may be skewing this value, and you have no data to correlate work performed by an individual vs estimated by a team. Unless you have a team of fairly equally skilled developers and they have been working together for a while, scrum point estimating is rarely accurate in my experience.

If the person doing the work is the one that estimates it, then you can gain an understanding of their estimation accuracy with each passing task, and make adjustments accordingly. It is important that developers are given the chance to do this, and do not go straight into scrum estimation in their careers.

4.18 Avoid large stakeholder meetings

Many of us have been there – sat in a meeting for 2 hours, with 10-15 other people, yet only 3 of them say anything of use. It is very typical at companies with 100 or more employees and a small internal development department.

Quite often, there will be management staff in attendance who have an interest in multiple projects, and tend to have problems scheduling prompt meetings or balancing a forever changing schedule. So meetings will get delayed until everyone is available, potentially delaying the project.

Yet quite often, these same people only really need to know if everything is going OK, or if something needs to be actioned to rectify a problem. For these people, your project management should provide a weekly 'traffic light' (aka RAG rating) report of the progress. This will state the high-level tasks underway and provide a simple red, amber or green status light next to each one. Green tasks are proceeding fine, amber ones highlight tasks that have been identified as potential imminent problems, and red ones are problems that need solving.

For normal weekly project meetings, the development staff, project manager and one or two stakeholders (maybe for only the first half of the meeting) is usually sufficient. For exceptional meetings (to address yellow/red items) – one or two developers, the project management, and the relevant stakeholders only should be present.

The fewer people you can have in a meeting, the easier it is to schedule and the shorter it can be.

4.19 Avoid too many stakeholder meetings

Similar to having meetings which are too large, is having meetings which are too frequent. A typical reaction to a project that has slipped behind schedule is for a manager to say 'ok, let's have a meeting twice a week to keep on top of it'

But what this usually achieved, is taking resources away from working on the problem, to talk about the problem instead. Needless to say, this is counterproductive, and yet it occurs all too often.

Instead, maybe a project manager needs to micro-manage part of the development team, to keep an eye on this specific problem, then report status and changes to those interested.

The more meetings you have, the less work you do.

4.20 Perform release and project retrospectives

At the end of a project (or an iterative development cycle), perform a retrospective. Look at what worked well or poorly (especially with respect to estimates and communications) and try to learn from the experience for subsequent releases. Do not spend too long on it, and do **not** ask developers to (for example) list three good things and three bad things. If they cannot think of three, then there were not three worth mentioning, so you will be collecting made-up or biased information. It is perfectly valid to have 'not learned anything new' or 'only this one thing was good' in such a retrospective.

4.21 Quality is not subjective

Some may argue that software quality is subjective. However, for the majority of business software, there is a fairly consistent list of qualities that developers and users should expect, which you should strive for on all projects:

- **Features** – the functions the software actually performs.
- **Speed** – how quickly the software responds. Reports, delays between screen changes etc.
- **Ease of Use** – it should be as intuitive as possible.
- **Stability** – does it crash or stop responding under load?
- **Security** – Appropriate levels of security built into the software to protect the client's data.
- **Determinism** – It should produce the same outputs, given the same inputs each time (also relates to ease of use)
- **Maintainability** – It should be well structured to facilitate maintenance.
- **Scalability** – Does the design allow for adding new functionality, or scaling up to additional load and hardware?
- **Documentation** – Both for the user and subsequent developers.

These qualities need to be considered and built in to the system from the group up, they cannot easily be retrofitted.

The client may not understand or appreciate all of these qualities – it is up to the analyst to determine the correct level of each, based on discussions with the client.

4.22 Use matching server environments

For client-server projects (for example, cloud or web-based applications), make sure that the development, testing and production server environments match each other.

It is quite common for software to work within its development environment, but fail when it is taken to the testing (or worse still, production) environment. Mismatched Operating Systems or versions, or system software package versions, even physical hardware differences, can cause an application to fail.

Many companies make some effort to keep their UAT environment as close as possible to their live setup, but many fail to make their development environments match. With the virtual machine technology available today, there is no real excuse for this.

Mismatched development and test/production environments cause a significant amount of time loss, yes are normally quite simple to fix.

4.23 Risks to project schedules

The following list represents the biggest risks to development project schedules:

- Bad or incomplete specifications
- Requirements changes
- Imposed time constraints
- Staff shortages
- Staff skills
- Too many stakeholders

Make it a point to continuously monitor these items and look for anything threatening your project. By actively keeping an eye on these items, you will be better placed to pro-actively address them, or stop them from adversely affecting your project.

5. Staff Management

This section is aimed at those who manage software development staff. Generic management advice is not covered here, only issues that relate specifically to software development staff.

Development staff, their managers, and project managers should read this section.

5.1 Support your developers

There will likely be occasions where development staff are under extreme pressure to complete some work (for example, fixing a bug affecting revenue on a live system). At times like this, you should support them and provide as much assistance as possible.

Enable them to stay focussed on the task at hand. Fetch them coffee, lunch, and remove non-essential daily distractions and chores from them.

Make sure they are not distracted by other members of staff, and especially from having to context switch on to other projects (see section 2.15 Avoid context switching).

If making complex changes or fixes, and/or performing these on a live system, provide another developer to sit with them (pairing). This provides an extra set of eyes to sanity check the work and also help spot human errors.

5.2 Quality staff, not quantity

Productivity can easily vary by a factor of ten between the best and worst development staff in any one company. In addition, the more staff involved in a project, the more cross-communication is required and subsequently productivity drops.

Although their productivity may vary by a factor of ten, their respective salaries will not. So you are likely to be better off hiring four excellent programmers than ten average ones.

Many companies will have one, maybe two 'star' programmers, and hope that they will mentor the less proficient ones. If your company tries to benefit from this setup, then monitor the results, as it is not always successful and will always be a drain on the productivity of your star developer, not to mention the fact it may lessen the enjoyment of the job for them and increase the chances of them leaving.

5.3 Perform code reviews

Code reviews are an excellent way to sustain code quality. They are also especially important for remote teams and for new staff. It is an excellent and inexpensive way of trapping errors and preventing poor code from entering your system.

Asking developers to inspect each other's code is an excellent way to stop programmers from being lazy and cutting corners, for fear of having their weak code discovered by someone else. 'Discovered' vs 'reported' is a critical factor here. It is important not to make code reviews a 'name and shame' session. They should be considered by your company and staff as sanity checks, and maybe looking for anything that has 'slipped through the cracks'. Developers naturally don't like having their code criticized by others, so the mere fact that someone else will be looking at it (without any expectation of apportioning blame), is usually sufficient to keep them from allowing poorly written code into the system.

It is also a good way to check the quality of code being produced by new members of staff, where you have no track record of quality.

However, it is also an extremely valuable tool for monitoring code produced by off-site (remote and/or outsourced) staff. For remote staff, you should initially aim for daily code submissions and reviews, and reduce that as your confidence grows.

5.4 Avoid multitasking across projects

Context switching is very expensive. Wherever possible you should avoid having developers working on more than one project. Try to keep the same staff working on a project until its completion.

Of course, there will be times where someone will need to work on something else, maybe an urgent bug from a previous project. But minimising the number of switches between projects can save you an enormous amount of productivity time (see section 2.15 Avoid context switching).

Balance this against ensuring your developers do get to work on as many different projects as possible. This will increase their skills, their motivation and also longevity in their job.

5.5 Software Developers need thinking space

The job of a software developer is substantially different from virtually all other office jobs. In most jobs, a person is tasked with several things to do. Some may last a few minutes, others an hour or two. Rarely they will last a whole day or more. However, most of these tasks will be fairly independent of each other, making it easy for that worker to perform some work, deal with a distraction, move on to the next item, and so on.

By contrast, the developer is working on a very large problem, broken down into many tasks. Each of these tasks are intricately associated with each other, and a lot of information has to be maintained in memory throughout the life-cycle of a particular piece of work, which may be several weeks.

Because of this, developers need to maintain concentration for long periods of time. Noisy environments and open offices can be extremely distracting, making concentration difficult. Allow developers to use headphones to block out office noise. Also allow remote working.

Developers also need time and space to think about their coding problems and to design coding solutions. For this, it helps to provide a relaxation or games room where staff can either think about the problems in a quiet place, or take their minds off them completely (which helps the subconscious find the solutions for them).

5.6 Outsource with care

Outsourcing parts of a project to an external agency can be an excellent way to reduce costs or bridge a skills gap, but exercise caution, as it requires tighter quality control checking on your part, and it's too convenient to skip on this important task.

This is by no means indicative of all outsourcing suppliers, but remember, as a separate entity, their goals are not truly aligned with yours. This means they will not care about the outcome of your project as much, or be fearful of any reprimands for poor work, like a direct employee would.

It is therefore imperative that, at least until you have built up a good working relationship and trust, that you check the quality and quantity of work on a daily basis, and do not wait, for example, for a module to be completed before being delivered.

5.7 Hire intelligence, not skill set

Many managers, when hiring programming staff, generally present a 'shopping list' of skills that they want prospective staff to have. However, this is the wrong approach.

The programming landscape is in constant flux. New languages, libraries, frameworks and even methodologies are popping up almost weekly. But these things are just 'tools' used by programmers, much the same as tools are used by a carpenter. A carpenter needs to learn his craft first, and then he can happily switch to using whatever tools become available in due course. No one tool will make him a better carpenter.

And so it is with programmers. If a programmer is intelligent, they will learn their craft, and will be able to adapt to new languages and technologies as they arise. But that fundamental skill of programming, being able to break down problems in to mathematical and logical blocks that a computer can interpret, transcends the languages, libraries, and tools available. Without that skill, any programmer is limited.

So the next time you are looking to hire developers, do not rely on a 'shopping list' of skills you would like, together with an arbitrary 'number of years experience' you feel appropriate for each. Look principally for intelligence, programming, and problem solving aptitude, ability to communicate clearly, and the ability to describe and discuss technical ideas in layman's terms.

5.8 Retaining development staff

It is not unusual for programming staff to leave a job after two years or so. This is typically because programmers want to keep learning new technologies and expand their skill set through experience. It also occurs because, if they are maintaining one principal project, the chances are that 'code rot' will set in (where more and more shortcuts have been taken, and unplanned features added that were not originally designed for) and the code has become harder to work with, making their day less enjoyable.

There are several things you can do to help retain your development staff:

- Give them varied projects to work on.
- Limit their time spent teaching juniors or educating users (though some developers enjoy this – find out!)
- Allow project re-writes.
- Allow them to learn and explore new languages and tools.
- Allow remote and/or flexitime working.

5.9 Ease developer staff turnover

It may simply be that your developer positions are not conducive enough to retain staff for long periods, despite any attempts you have made to sweeten the deal.

When the work itself just isn't going to be challenging, changing or diverse enough to retain staff long term, embrace the process of staff turnover instead.

Make sure your systems are well defined, that you have a wiki filled with details of hardware and software configuration details, that your induction process to get a new starter both set up with hardware and also the tool-chain and code base, is as streamlined as possible, and that your code base is well structured with readability and maintainability high on your priorities list, to lessen the time needed to bring a new person up to speed.

5.10 There is no 'one size fits all' solution.

Remember, no one tool, language, framework or process is completely ideal for you. Do not insist all development is done in one language. If you adopt (for example) agile methodology or ITIL, do not necessarily adopt all of their processes. If you use a project management tool, do not force yourself to use every component or feature.

Cherry pick what works for you, and keep everything as lean as possible. The only thing that shouldn't be lean is your documentation on how, what and why.

6. Acronyms

The following acronyms occur frequently in software development. These terms are also described in the following glossary.

API	Application Programming Interface
BAU	Business As Usual
BCP	Business Continuity Planning
BDD	Behaviour Driven Development
CD	Continuous Delivery
CD	Continuous Deployment
CI	Continuous Integration
DR	Disaster Recovery
ERD	Entity Relationship Diagram
IaaS	Infrastructure as a Service
IDE	Integrated Development Environment
ITIL	Information Technology Infrastructure Library
JSON	JavaScript Object Notation
OOA	Object Oriented Analysis
OOD	Object Oriented Design
OOP	Object Oriented Programming
PaaS	Platform as a Service
QA	Quality Assurance

RAG	Red Amber Green
SaaS	Software as a Service
SDK	Software Development Kit
SDLC	Software Development Life-cycle
SDM	Software Development Methodology
SSADM	Structured Systems Analysis and Design Method
TCO	Total Cost of Ownership
TDD	Test Driven Design
UAT	User Acceptance Testing
UI	User Interface
UML	Unified Modelling Language
UX	User Experience
VCS	Version Control System
XML	Extensible Markup Language
XP	Extreme Programming

7. Glossary of Terms

The following terms are mentioned in this book and/or in software development in general.

3-tier application

The 3-tier architecture is the most common of the multi-tier (or n-tier) client-server architectures, in which the presentation, application logic and data storage functions (tiers) are physically separated. The client is the web browser, providing the presentation (UI) tier, and the server side is typically split in to two tiers, one to handle the application logic, and another to handle database/storage.

Agile Software Development

A set of principles for software development advocating adaptive planning, evolutionary development, early delivery, continuous improvement, and rapid and flexible response to change. These principles are used by an increasing number of more modern software development methods.

Analyst Programmer

A person who performs two roles: one of requirements analysis and software design, and also of computer programmer (or developer), who writes the code according to the specifications provided.

Application Programming Interface (API)

An API is a set of protocols that allows an application to interface to (that is, to make use of) the features of another system or subsystem (the one which is providing the API). For example, a website might make use of a weather API provided by a meteorological office to provide and display weather forecasts.

Black box testing

This involves creating unit tests for a given module without knowing anything of its implementation, working solely from the specifications which define the module's inputs and outputs.

Bug

A defect in software.

Bug Tracking System

A software tool for recording, monitoring, and updating those concerned with the status of bugs found in a software application (or applications), including issues, fixes, workarounds and eventual solving.

Build

A version of software that has been compiled from its various sources and elements, to create a distributable version of a software product. Build numbers are often used as a third component in a produced version number, e.g. version 1.2 build 5678 (or 1.2.5678).

Build Server

A build server, also called a continuous integration server (CI server), is a centralized environment for building distributed development projects.

Business Analyst

A person who performs requirements analysis, simplification, translation, planning and documentation on behalf of the client, so that the software design can support the business requirements.

Business As Usual

A term to denote the normal conduct of operations within a

business, despite any events or circumstances that might affect it negatively. Some computing jobs may be tasked with maintaining BAU. A disaster recovery plan may refer to time needed to restore BAU. Maintaining Business As Usual is the goal of Business Continuity Planning (BCP).

Business Continuity Planning

The creation of systems and processes of prevention and recovery to support a business' ongoing operations (Business As Usual). BCP should be considered during any systems software design, to try to minimise any potential loss of data, system downtime and disaster recovery time.

Behaviour Driven Development

This is an extension of Test Driven Development, whereby the specifications for a system are created using Domain Specific Language and natural language sentences, to create 'user stories' and 'scenarios'. These user stories each identify a stakeholder, a business effect and a business value, plus one or more scenarios, each with a precondition, trigger and expected outcome(s).

Change control

A systematic approach to managing all changes made to a product or system, to ensure that all changes are documented, existing services are not unnecessarily disrupted, and resources are assigned appropriately.

Client

The person or company paying for, and providing the specifications for, the software under development. The client may or may not also be the customer.

Code coverage report

A report detailing the amount of software code that is 'covered' by (i.e. is execute by) a respective test suite. Ideally 100% of code would be covered, but it is typical for companies to settle on 75-85% of subroutines or functions, and 75-85% of program lines to be covered.

Code review

The practice of asking one developer to check the code written by another, usually as part of a quality control process. Also referred to as a peer review.

Cohesion

Refers to the relationship of different pieces of functionality within any one software module. The more closely related the functions are within a given module, the higher its cohesion. Modules of higher cohesion are more desirable as they are typically more reliable, re-usable and understandable.

Context switching

A context switch generally means switching from one task to another, and is how computers and humans appear to multitask. In human terms, context switching is very expensive (especially when the tasks are software development), and can lower productivity to as little as 20%.

Continuous Delivery (CD)

CD builds upon Continuous Integration. Whereas CI deals with the build and test part of the development process, CD creates a valid release or system build from the committed code, ready to deploy in to production systems.

Continuous Deployment (CD)

Continuous Deployment is the furtherance of Continuous Delivery, whereby the production-ready build (or release) is automatically deployed in to the live environment.

Continuous Integration (CI)

A software engineering practice in which isolated changes are immediately tested and reported on when they are committed back to the code base. The goal of CI is to provide rapid feedback so that if a defect is introduced into the code base, it can be identified and corrected as soon as possible. Continuous integration software tools can be used to automate the testing and reporting.

Coupling

Coupling refers to the extent at which one module, function or class relies on the internal workings of another. High coupling occurs when one function relies on knowledge of another's inner workings (e.g. sharing of global data). Low coupling occurs when one function is able to communicate with another using a very narrow and specific interface (e.g. passing parameters or messages). Loosely-coupled systems are generally better designed and easier to maintain.

Customer

The end-user of the software. This may or may not be the client (the one who owns and pays for the software).

Data Modelling

Data Modelling is the first step in database and object-oriented design, where the designer creates a conceptual model of how data items (or objects) relate to each other, before converting this into a physical database schema.

Debugging

The process of finding and removing bugs (defects) from software. The term is thought to have come from the earliest mechanical computers and complex mechanical machines, which produced errors when bugs got caught up in their moving parts. Removing the bugs ('debugging') the system referred literally to the process of looking for, and removing, bugs.

Defect Tracking

See Bug Tracking

Deprecated

In IT, deprecation refers to something that, although is allowed or available, is not recommended for use. The term may be used with almost any element of IT, including software, hardware, methods, models and practices. For example, an old, unsupported version of an Operating System, or some language functions which have been superseded by newer functions and are earmarked for eventual removal.

Design Pattern

In software engineering parlance, a design pattern is a recognised, repeatable solution to a common programming problem, in the same way that a cam and a hinge are design patterns in mechanical engineering.

Developer

A person who writes, or develops, software. Another term for a software programmer.

Disaster Recovery (DR)

A plan to put in motion for the restoration or continuation of vital infrastructure or systems following any one of several anticipated disasters.

Downtime

The amount of time a system or piece of infrastructure has been unavailable.

Entity Relationship Diagram

An ERD is a graphical representation of the relationship between objects, events or concepts within a system, and is often used as a data modelling tool to define a system's relational database structure.

Extensible Markup Language (XML)

A markup language that defines a set of rules to represent any data in a format which is both human-readable and machine-readable. Whilst still popular for large scale data interchanges between different systems, smaller web-based API's have largely switched to the more streamlined JSON format.

Extreme Programming

An agile development methodology, which promotes short development cycles, a flat management structure, pair programming, and thorough unit testing.

Feature Creep

A common tendency for functional requirements to increase whilst the software product is still in development. This can lead to code quality issues and schedule overruns.

Framework

A software framework is a set of libraries and other code, which provide a subsystem into which application software can be developed. Such frameworks speed development by providing pre-written code to handle low-level functions, and aid maintainability and stability by promoting a well-defined structure to the application code.

Functional Specifications

A document that describes in detail the features, capabilities, user interfaces, machine interfaces and other requirements of a software system.

GANTT Chart

A type of bar chart used in project management. On the left side is a list of tasks that need to be completed, and across the top is a time scale. Bars against each task identify the expected start and end times of each task.

Greenfield Project

A new software project, analogous to the construction industry, where building on greenfield land is unimpeded by existing infrastructure.

Grey box testing

A strategy for software testing where the tester has limited knowledge of the internal workings of the code under test. Grey box testing is considered to be non-intrusive and unbiased, as it does not require access to the source code. The tester may know how the individual system units should interact, but has no knowledge of their internal workings. Contrast this with white box and black box testing.

Hotfix

The term used for a software patch that is to be applied to a live (aka 'hot' or 'production') system, usually to fix a problem considered critical enough to bypass the normal development and testing cycles.

Impact Analysis

The evaluation of the effects on resources, schedule, effort and risks that would be caused by a software change.

Information Technology Infrastructure Library

ITIL is a set of best practices standards for information technology (IT) service management. It allows companies to demonstrate compliance and measure their improvement.

Integrated Development Environment

A software application that provides multiple tools to aid a developer in writing software. In addition to a code editor, an IDE may contain built-in language documentation and syntax checking, build automation tools, version control, debugging tools and more.

Iterative Development

An agile planning and development process where software is developed in small sections (iterations). After each iteration, the customer can view the product and steer subsequent development accordingly.

JavaScript Object Notation (JSON)

Pronounced 'JASON', it is a text-based, human-readable data interchange format used for representing simple data structures and objects in both JavaScript code and in web-based API services. Although part of the JavaScript language, JavaScript is not required in its use.

Kanban board

A visual project management tool whereby tasks are placed in to one of several columns and progress from left to right. The actual columns may vary but typically include: backlog, ready, in development, in testing, in UAT, ready for deployment, deployed. Additional features may exist, such as WIP (Work In Progress) limits for each column, and multiple 'swim-lanes' across all columns (used to divide the board for different projects, etc).

Lean Programming

A development approach inspired from lean manufacturing, which follows seven general principles: eliminate waste, build quality in, create knowledge, defer commitment, deliver fast, respect people, optimise the whole.

Man hours

A unit of measurement for stating how long a task will take, not counting breaks and interruptions.

N-tier

N-tier applications break up applications in to self-contained sections (the most common format being 3-tier, see earlier). These tiers can be split across software or hardware only, or both. The advantage being that one tier can be easily changed, upgraded, made more performant, etc., without impacting the other tiers.

Object Oriented Analysis / Design

OOA and OOD refer to the practice of planning and designing a series of interacting objects, that represent the real world problem that the software is trying to solve. For example,

Object Oriented Programming

A programming paradigm based on the concept of objects. Objects typically contain data (called attributes) and functions (called methods), and the attributes can only be manipulated through the object's methods (called encapsulation). This is one of the key concepts of OOP.

Open Source

The term given to software whose source code is freely obtainable. Open Source Software is typically 'free' software, meaning it can be obtained without cost.

Outsourcing

Derived from the term 'outside resourcing', it is the practice of contracting out a business process to a third party. Many companies outsource their software development, at least in part.

Pair programming

An agile software development technique whereby two programmers sit at one computer. One writes the code while the other observes and checks, and they both discuss. The pair may or may not take it in turns to write the code.

Peer review

see *Code review*

Presentation Layer

See *User Interface*

Product Life-cycle

The product life-cycle is the collective stages that a product goes through from its conception and design through to its ultimate disposal.

Product Owner

Product owner is a scrum development role for a person who represents the business or user community and is responsible for working with the user group to determine what features will be in the product release.

Programmer

See *Developer*

Project manager

The person who manages a software project.

Prototyping

A systems development method in which a prototype is built, then repeatedly tested and modified. Once the essential functionality works as desired, it can be further developed into a fully functioning piece of software.

Pseudocode

A detailed but human-readable description of what a computer program or algorithm must do, expressed in a formally-styled yet natural language, thereby avoiding any specialist knowledge to understand it.

Quality Assurance

In software development terms, the QA process is essentially any element of software testing, such as unit tests, automated tests, manual code reviews, and continuous integration.

RAG Rating

Also known as a Traffic Light Rating, this is a popular method of quickly highlighting the status of project issues or tasks with a visual colour reference. Green denotes OK, Amber denotes a warning and Red highlights problems.

Refactoring

A process of re-structuring the internal workings of a unit of code without affecting its external behaviour.

Regression testing

The retesting of previously tested code modules to ensure that defects have not been introduced or uncovered as a result of changes made.

Requirements Analysis

Requirements analysis, also called requirements engineering, is the process of determining user expectations for a new or modified product. These features, called requirements, must be quantifiable, relevant and detailed. In software engineering, such requirements are often called functional specifications. Requirements analysis is an important aspect of project management.

Requirements Specifications

The documentation produced by performing Requirements Analysis.

Response times

How quickly a computer, an API, or other piece of software code responds to a request.

SCRUM

Scrum is an agile software development framework whose key principle is to understand the customers will likely change their mind during development. Scrum works in iterative cycles and aims to deliver incrementally and respond to changing requirements.

Server

A computer which is (usually) dedicated to providing (serving) a particular service, such as a print server, file server, or in the case of client-server applications, a web server and database server. Such servers are normally left operational 24/7 and are hardened against failure.

Server Load

The amount of work a server is currently doing, normally expressed as a fraction of 1 per CPU. A dual CPU server at load average of 1 is 50% busy.

Smoke Testing

Refers to a group of basic, non-exhaustive tests which verify that the basic functionality of the software under test remains valid. It is often performed as a pre-cursor to more in-depth tests.

Software as a Service (SaaS)

This is a software distribution model in which a third-party provider hosts applications and makes them available to customers over the Internet. SaaS is one of three main categories of cloud computing, alongside infrastructure as a service (IaaS) and platform as a service (PaaS).

Software Configuration Management

SCM is the task of tracking, controlling, reporting, monitoring and auditing of changes in software. It requires Version Control and the tracking of working baseline configurations. Should a change go wrong, SCM can identify what was changed, when and by who, and can 'roll back' to a previous working baseline.

Software Development Kit

A collection of software tools and documentation that eases or allows the creation of software for a particular software framework, hardware platform, or computer system.

Software Development Life Cycle

The division of software development into distinct stages with the intent to improve planning and management. Typical methodologies include prototyping, waterfall, various types of agile, extreme programming, incremental and iterative.

Software Development Methodology

See *Software Development Life-cycle*

Software Library

A software library is a collection of code modules that provide pre-written functionality for commonly-required features, speeding software development.

Source Control

See *Version Control*

Sprint

In software development, a sprint is a (usually) set period of time during which specific work has to be completed and made ready for review.

Each sprint begins with a planning meeting. During the meeting, the product owner (the person requesting the work) and the development team agree upon exactly what work will be accomplished during the sprint. The development team has the final say when it comes to determining how much work can realistically be accomplished during the sprint, and the product owner has the final say on what criteria need to be met for the work to be approved and accepted.

Staging environment

A computer system that is set up to mirror a live production environment as closely as possible, that is used to test software (typically UAT) prior to deployment.

Stakeholder

A project stakeholder is a person or entity that has an interest in the activity or outcome of a project. Everyone mentioned in this book is a stakeholder.

Stress Testing

Testing conducted to evaluate a system or module, either at or beyond the limits of its specified requirements, so see how it responds.

Structured Programming

A subset of procedural programming that enforces a logical

structure to make it easier to understand and modify.

Structured Systems Analysis And Design Method

SSADM is a waterfall method for building software systems, and can be considered the latest and greatest of SDM's that are heavily document-led, in contrast to the agile methods that have since gained more popularity.

System Testing

The process of testing an integrated system to verify that it meets specified requirements, covering both functional and non-functional system testing.

Test Driven Development

A software development methodology which states that for each unit of software, a software developer must:

- Define a set of tests for that unit.
- Create the structure of the unit (all tests will fail).
- Implement the unit details so that it passes all tests

Test Environment

See *Staging environment*

Test Plan

A test plan documents the strategy that will be used to verify and ensure that a product or system meets its design specifications and other requirements.

Test Script

A set of instructions to be performed on a system under test to determine whether it functions as expected. Test scripts can be manually executed or automated.

Total Cost of Ownership

A financial calculation or estimate intended to buyers or owners to determine both the direct and indirect costs of any product or system.

Unified Modelling Language

UML is a general purpose modelling language, designed to help visualise a system's architecture.

Unit test

A testing mechanism where individual pieces of code are testing in isolation from other parts, in order to determine whether they function correctly.

Uptime

The amount of time a server or particular service has been in operation. Common targets are measured in 'nines' - 3 nines be 99.9%, four nines being 99.99% and five nines being 99.999%.

User Acceptance Testing (UAT)

A phase of software development in which the software is tested in the "real world" by the intended audience.

User Experience (UX)

UX refers to a user's emotions and perceptions when using a software products' user interface. A good user experience will be intuitive and easy for a user to operate, while a bad experience may leave a user frustrated and unable to achieve their intended goals.

User Interface (UI)

In software terms the UI is where the user interacts with the computer. Typically this is in the form of a display to show the data, and various input mechanisms for the user to modify and add data to the screen.

Version Control System

Version Control (or Source Control) Systems form a vital tool used by development teams. They enable changes to source (or any other type of file) to be recorded and recalled at will. This makes it easy for developers to change code, and revert back to previous versions. Some systems also facilitate the 'merging' of work from two or more developers on the same files.

Virtual Server

A server that runs as a program within another, physical, server. Virtual Servers are used by developers to mimic the intended production environment, as well as by companies (in either private or public 'clouds') due to their ease of management and flexibility compared to physical servers.

Waterfall Model

A development model that rigidly defines a linear structure to development, starting with full specifications and ending with delivery of the final product. This development model is giving way to more agile and responsive models.

White box testing

Software testing that is based on the knowledge of the internal structure of the component under test. Also known as glass box testing.

XML

See Extensible Markup Language

www.ingramcontent.com/pod-product-compliance
Lightning Source LLC
Chambersburg PA
CBHW071216050326
40689CB00011B/2335